When Your Comfort Zone Gets the Squeeze

Charles R. Swindoll

*T*o most people pain is an enemy... nothing more than an invading, adversary force that takes unfair advantage of its victims. Stop and think. Who ever thought of affliction as a friend? How many folks do you know who would encourage you to learn from God's messages, even though they come wrapped in discomfort?

This booklet approaches the subject of adversity from that point of view. It approaches the subject realistically, not mystically. These pages are based on the scriptural suggestion that we are not to be disturbed and demoralized when our comfort zone gets the squeeze. Why? Because during and following those times of distress, our God deposits some of His best lessons into our lives.

So then, as you read what I have written, take time to put *yourself* in the scene. Think of your particular circumstances, especially those that seem unusually difficult. Ask the Lord to give you the patience and the perspective to glean much wisdom as you apply what you are reading.

May you *grow* rather than simply *groan* through it all!

We sent Timothy... to strengthen and encourage you as to your faith, so that no man may be disturbed by these afflictions; for you yourselves know that we have been destined for this.

1 THESSALONIANS 3:2,3

When Your Comfort Zone Gets the Squeeze

Physician Scott Peck calls it "the road less traveled." Scholar C. S. Lewis refers to it as "God's megaphone." Contemporary author Philip Yancey says that it is "the gift nobody wants." English poet Byron referred to it as "the path to truth." But no one ever said it better than Isaac Watts. While writing the lyrics for a hymn that Christians still sing today, he asked direct and searching questions: "Am I a soldier of the cross, a follower of the Lamb?" And again, "Must I be carried to the skies on flowery beds of ease, while others fought to win the prize and sailed thru bloody seas?"

What is this "road less traveled"? Where is that "path to truth"? I'm referring to pain. It's in pain that God speaks to us through His megaphone. *Suffering* is "the road less traveled." *Affliction* is "the path to truth." *Hardship* and *adversity*—these are the gifts nobody wants. Just the presence of these things in our lives creates tension.

For example, you go to your physician for an annual checkup. He takes your X ray. Within a few days he contacts you and says, "We'll need to do a biopsy." After the biopsy, he faces you with that horrible piece of information: you have cancer. There's no getting around it. Enter: high-level tension.

One part of us responds, "I will accept this. There is no such thing as a mistake in the life of the child of God. This is a 'road less traveled,' and I want to travel it carefully and well. I want to learn all that God is saying to me through this affliction."

But another part of us says, "I will fight this to the end, because I am a survivor and because I believe there may well be a cure around the corner. So I will not succumb. I will not lie down in my bed, give up hope, and die an early death."

It is the tension between acceptance and resistance. The conflict is actually a mental struggle between seeing God as a God of sovereign control and viewing Him as a God of gracious mercy. There are lessons to be learned that can only be learned along the road of affliction, hardship, and pain.

Suffering Is Inevitable

There's no getting around it, pain and suffering are inevitable. Our parents did not escape it, you and I will not escape it, and neither will our children. According to Philippians 1:29, suffering is here to stay.

For to you it has been granted for Christ's sake, not only to believe in Him, but also to suffer for His sake.

There are some today who say, "All suffering is wrong. All who suffer are out of the will of God. If you suffer, you are in sin. And since you are in sin, if you will deal correctly and sufficiently with your sin, your suffering will go away." That is simply not the truth. Scripture does not support such teaching. To be sure, all suffering is rooted in the fact that sin has entered the human race; however, not only has it been granted that we believe in Christ, but it has also been planned that we suffer.

Second Corinthians 4:7-10 presents a similar set of facts:

But we have this treasure in earthen vessels, that the surpassing greatness of the power may be of God and not from ourselves; we are afflicted in every way, but not crushed; perplexed, but not despairing; persecuted, but not forsaken; struck down, but not destroyed; always carrying about in the body the dying of Jesus, that the life of Jesus also may be manifested in our body.

This represents one of the deep mysteries of God. By *"carrying about in the body the dying of Jesus,"* we enter into the true lifestyle of Christ—real living.

A few verses later in 2 Corinthians 4, we read,

Therefore we do not lose heart, but though our outer man is decaying, yet our inner man is being renewed day by day (v. 16).

Again, notice we are decaying. And yet deep within we are being renewed.

First Peter 4:12-13 assures us that suffering should never surprise us.

Beloved, do not be surprised at the fiery ordeal among you, which comes upon

*you for your testing, as though some
strange thing were happening to you; but
to the degree that you share the
sufferings of Christ, keep on rejoicing; so
that also at the revelation of His glory,
you may rejoice with exultation.*

Look at that, Christian! Are you, right this
moment in your life, being reviled? Are you
currently under attack as a soldier of the cross?
Here's a new way to look at such treatment:
You are blessed! Rejoice! It's part of the
package. It is inevitable.

*By no means let any of you suffer as a
murderer, or thief, or evildoer, or a
troublesome meddler; but if anyone
suffers as a Christian, let him not feel
ashamed, but in that name let him
glorify God* (vv. 15-16).

Now that's one side of the coin. Suffering is
inevitable.

Pain Is Essential

There's another side to this same
coin ... and that's the part that says suffering
and pain are also essential. In Psalm 119 there
are three verses separated from each other but
connected by the same thought—Psalm 119:67,
71, and 75.

*Before I was afflicted I went astray, but
now I keep Thy word. . . . It is good for
me that I was afflicted, that I may learn
Thy statutes. . . . I know, O Lord, that
Thy judgments are righteous, and that in
faithfulness Thou hast afflicted me.*

A man told me recently, "God never had my
attention until He laid me on my back. Since

then, I've been listening!" This strong-willed and stubborn man was fighting back the tears as he spoke those words. And he's only been in the crucible less than two weeks.

Suffering is essential if we hope to become effective for God. A. W. Tozer said it like this: "It is doubtful whether God can bless a man greatly until He has hurt him deeply."[1]

Solomon, in his journal named Ecclesiastes, wrote:

Consider the work of God, for who is able to straighten what He has bent? In the day of prosperity be happy, but in the day of adversity consider—God has made the one as well as the other . . . (7:13-14).

"Consider." In Hebrew, the term means "to inspect." It was used by Moses in Exodus 3, verse 3. When the bush began to burn, he said, in effect, "I will now turn aside and *consider* why the bush is not consumed." It was his way of saying, "I will make an investigation." The term includes the idea of perceiving. And when it is used of oneself, it's the idea of revealing to oneself the truth, examining for the purpose of evaluating.

Let's go back.

Consider the work of God, for who is able to straighten what He has bent? In the day of prosperity be happy, but in the day of adversity consider [inspect, examine, gain some objective instruction, slow down and listen]—*God has made the one as well as the other. . . .*

Suffering is essential, not only because it softens our spirits, making us sensitive to the voice of God, but also because it reveals to us the true nature of ourselves. It shows us the truth about ourselves.

Although this journey along the avenue of affliction is unpleasant and unappealing, it is both inevitable and essential. No one in God's family can remain a stranger to pain and suffering.

An Ancient Example

Centuries ago, there was a fine group of Christians in the Macedonian church at Thessalonica. The man who was responsible for founding that church wrote them a letter of encouragement when he heard of the hard times they were enduring. Even though his missionary travels forced him to press on into other regions, his heart was still moved over their plight ... so he sent his capable companion, Timothy, to check up on how they were doing.

Unable to get them off his mind, the Apostle Paul decided to have his friend travel back to Thessalonica and determine the truth of what he'd been hearing. He wondered how they were doing in the storm of suffering that had followed his departure. He had been concerned about them long enough. It was time for action. The opening statement of 1 Thessalonians 3 reveals his plan:

> *Therefore when we could endure it no longer, we thought it best to be left behind at Athens alone; and we sent Timothy our brother* [to find out how you're doing]. . . .

If one of your kids attended Kent State University or was a student at the University of California in Berkeley in the late 1960s, you understand such concern. If you had a son or daughter in the Vietnam War in the late '60s and early '70s, you understand the *"therefore"* of chapter 3, verse 1.

There is something about being in a context that is marked by panic and adversity and the vicious treatment of individuals that causes you as a parent to be uneasy. You don't sleep well. You mentally imagine what they're going through. And you, on occasion, find yourself unable to endure. You have to have information about how your son or your daughter is doing.

Exactly what was it Timothy was sent to do? Paul states that he sent Timothy for two reasons: (1) to strengthen the believers and (2) to encourage them, as to their faith.

To help you understand the importance of those reasons, let's briefly examine those two terms. The word *"strengthen"* means "to shore up, to buttress." That's an old word we don't use today—"buttress." One man says, "It's to put a ramrod down one's back to enable him to stand straight and erect, come what may."

"I sent Timothy to put a ramrod down your back, so that you wouldn't slump and shuffle around as though you were being mistreated but would stand tall during the hard times . . . you'd stand erect, like a steer in a blizzard. You'd refuse to bend against the odds. I sent him to add strength to you."

They taught us in the marines that when you are preparing for combat, you should dig a hole big enough for two. There's nothing quite like fighting a battle all alone. There's something strengthening about having a buddy with you in battle that keeps you from panic. Paul says, "You needed somebody alongside to buttress you, to keep you from surrendering."

Now the second word, *"encourage,"* is a comforting word. *Parakaleō* is the Greek term. We get the word "Paraclete" from it, one of the titles of the Holy Spirit. It's often translated "comfort" in the New Testament, but here it is rendered *"encourage."* It is the idea of standing alongside another person to put courage into him or her. There is a loving, confident hug of reassurance in the word.

If you have ever gone through the valley, perhaps you could testify that you were able to make it only because a Timothy came to your side. Timothy, in your case, might have been a physician or a counselor or a neighbor or perhaps your own parents. But when the Timothy came, whoever he was, he brought strength and courage to you.

Notice, the encouragement had a target— to *"encourage you as to your faith."* Timothy didn't come just to say, "Buck up! You can handle it! Suck it up—that's the way it is in life! Others have made it and you can too!" He didn't come to be a motivational cheerleader. That's not it. Timothy came to examine and to help strengthen the Thessalonians in their faith.

Let me show you an example of this from the Old Testament, back in 1 Samuel 23. One of my favorite stories, when it comes to relationships, is about Jonathan and David. Young David was hunted by King Saul. Saul was in this crazed state of mind. The paranoid king was convinced that young David was trying to usurp the throne, so Saul forgot all about fighting Philistines and decided his greater need was to fight David, and ultimately to kill him. But in the meantime, Jonathan, Saul's son, had developed a warm and supportive relationship with David, his brother in the faith. Imagine the scene:

> And David stayed in the wilderness in the strongholds, and remained in the hill country in the wilderness of Ziph. And Saul sought him every day, but God did not deliver him into his hand. Now David became aware that Saul had come out to seek his life while David was in the wilderness of Ziph at Horesh (vv. 14-15).

You know, it's bad enough to have somebody on your tail, but it's even worse when you *find out* that they are. News reached David in his hiding place: "Saul is out to get you. He's got his men searching for you. They know what you look like. You'd better watch out." Look what happened according to the next verse:

> And Jonathan, Saul's son, arose and went to David at Horesh, and encouraged him in God (v. 16).

You talk about meeting a need! Jonathan became David's single source of earthly support. Stop and imagine how much David treasured that meeting with Jonathan.

We would be amazed if we could find out who the Davids are today. Feeling overwhelmed and pressured, one former pastor's wife in the Northeast writes: "My husband and I have occasionally felt on the edge of an ill-defined despair. Those were times when we felt a variety of things: a desire to either quit or run, a feeling of anger, the temptation to fight back at someone, the sense of being used or exploited, the weakness of inadequacy, and the reality of loneliness." She adds, "Such attitudes can easily conspire to reduce the strongest and the most gifted to a state of nothingness."[2]

Now back to the Thessalonians' situation. They needed a Timothy...a century-one Jonathan.

> *For this reason, when I could endure it no longer, I also sent to find out about your faith*... (1 Thess. 3:5a).

Remember, it wasn't just to see how they were doing. It wasn't a nosy curiosity—"I wanted to see how you were doing." Then, why?

> ... *for fear that the tempter might have tempted you, and our labor should be in vain* (v. 5b).

That is so practical!

One of the great battles within young Christians occurs when the adversary strikes during a time of suffering. The adversary finds that weak link or that chink in the armor, and he pushes his way in. That's when our comfort zone *really* gets the squeeze!

"When you can't endure it any longer, you pick up the phone and you call." That's a modern-day paraphrase of verse 5, I guess we can say. "When I could endure it no longer, I sent a friend. I wrote a letter. I took time from my schedule to check up on how you were doing."

We're not isolated islands of solid granite, living out our lives like rocks of Gibraltar. We are eroding pieces of soil on the seashore, especially when we are traveling the road of pain. When those age-old waves of affliction are beating against us, we need each other! Timothy's presence must have been a great encouragement to the Thessalonian believers.

Let me add here that on occasion it's wise to trace your churnings. Sometimes you will churn over someone during the night. When you awaken, you'll still be churning over the same individual . . . just can't seem to get the person out of your mind.

This was Paul's situation. *"When I could endure it no longer, I also sent to find out."* Want a little advice for no extra charge? *Don't ignore your churnings.* Trace them. Ask yourself why. Why can't I get so-and-so off my mind? Check up and find out! At the heart of Paul's concern was a *"fear that the tempter might have tempted you, and our labor should be in vain."* Paul didn't want to look back and say, "All of those hours we spent together were spent in vain."

Theological Perspective

To keep the right perspective in all of this, we need a solid dose of theology. Back to verses 3 and 4—same chapter, same subject of suffering. Paul has been concerned about the Thessalonians. Look at the theology behind the suffering. He sent Timothy to encourage, to strengthen them, *"so that no man may be disturbed by these afflictions . . ."* (v. 3a).

Before I go any further, I want to analyze that first part of verse 3. Paul states a fact that we can rely on. It is this: *Affliction need not unsettle God's people.*

A very interesting Greek term translated *"disturbed"* is used only here in all of the New Testament. Paul draws it from extrabiblical literature and has inserted it here, under the guidance of the Holy Spirit, to grab the attention of the reader.

Originally it was used to describe the wagging of a dog's tail. The whole idea was "to be shaken back and forth." The term later grew to mean more than the idea of a dog's wagging its tail. Finally, as you come up closer to it, the creature *bites!* And if you are a runner, you know exactly what I'm talking about. Rule number one ... never trust a dog that wags its tail. Why? It's gonna bite ya! It's going to catch you off guard. AND YOU'RE GOING TO BE DECEIVED! That's the word here.

"I don't want you, in the midst of the wagging of all of this experience, to be bitten, shaken, and hurt." A child of God need not be unsettled by affliction.

You know how it happens? It often begins with *questions.* See if these sound familiar: Doesn't God care about me anymore? Isn't He the One who promised to help me? How can He be good and permit this to happen to me? Why doesn't He answer my prayer—is He deaf? And then it intensifies into *doubt:* Maybe I've believed wrongly all my life. These questions cause us to start rethinking our bottom-line convictions.

Do you know somebody who's struggling through those thoughts right now? You know why they are? They have been *deceived* by affliction.

Paul realized how subtle the enemy is, so he dispatched Timothy. "I sent him to strengthen and encourage you, so that you wouldn't be full of doubt from these afflictions." That's the idea.

Now there is a logical and practical question we would be wise to ask: How can I keep from being disturbed by affliction? How can I keep from having those doubts that unsettle my faith? First of all, I remember that I have been destined for this.

> . . . so that no man may be disturbed by these afflictions; for you yourselves know that we have been destined for this (v. 3).

God, in His sovereign and inscrutable plan, realized that pain had to be a part of our training program, so He destined it for us.

And, second, I keep in mind that I have been warned ahead of time. Look at verse 4:

> For indeed when we were with you, we kept telling you in advance that we were going to suffer affliction; and so it came to pass, as you know.

As I mention warning someone about something important in advance, I recall a familiar scene. I prepared my two older children for marriage as best I could. And one of my pieces of counsel was this: Falling in love is wonderful. Courtship is great. The wedding ceremony is a memory you'll never forget. The honeymoon is . . . well, it's *pretty good!* But when all of that has taken place and you begin to live the real life, roll up your sleeves and tighten your belt. It's tough. So when they go— not if, but *when* they go—through the difficulties in marriage, they have been forewarned. Both have thanked me, by the way, for the previous "warning."

By being forewarned, we are forearmed to handle the pressures and challenges of married life. It helps to have some advance warning.

It's the same in the Christian life. There's no reason to be scandalized or shocked, because we have been warned ahead of time—unless you were led to Christ and discipled by someone who told you a lie; namely, "Trust Christ and all your problems will be solved." Then you are in for a real shocker! But if you have been faithfully and realistically trained, you have been equipped to handle this part of God's training program. You can stand firm through your journey along the avenue of affliction. When your comfort zone gets the squeeze, you're not blown away. You can handle it with remarkable inner peace.

By the way, you can't if you don't have Christ. Without Christ, you can no more enter into this life that I'm describing than you can fly by flapping your arms. In order for there to be that ramrod in your back, in order for you to be able to stand firm against times of adversity, Christ must remain in first place. And before that can occur, it is essential that you have the Lord Jesus in your life. That isn't automatic simply because you were born into a Christian home. You aren't a Christian just because you have moved into a Christian community or because you attend a church that preaches the truth of the gospel. You individually and independently must make that decision on your own. Only then can you *know* you're in God's family. And only then can you take life's blows on the chin without being knocked out.

Reactions to Affliction

You see, when we succumb to those overwhelming feelings of adversity, we tend to have three very normal and human reactions: first, resentment toward a former authority figure; second, isolation from Christian friends; and third, indifference regarding former teaching—we begin to doubt what we were once taught.

Interestingly, all three of those feelings were withstood by the Thessalonians. *"But now . . ."* See the contrast? "I was concerned. I sent Timothy. *But now* Timothy has come back, and he's brought us good news of your faith and love."

Isn't that just like Paul? The man was never petty. He was never nosy. He was sincerely concerned about how they were coming along in their walk with Christ. And he says, "You're doing great." How affirming!

Now note: *". . . and that you always think kindly of us . . ."* (v. 6). You might think, why did he put that in there? Because one of the signs of a twisted response to affliction is resenting a former authority. Guess who gets the business when a Christian in a congregation defects? The defecting Christian will often come back at the teacher. Sometimes it's the pastor. Sometimes it's the one who counseled him or her. But the Thessalonians didn't respond in that way. "I got word that you still love me! You still think kindly of me." So they passed the first test; they weren't resentful of Paul. "I'm encouraged to know that you still think kindly of us. You *always* think kindly of us, so you're doing well. You refuse to blame me for what you're going through."

They also passed the second test ... remember the second reaction? It's the tendency to isolate oneself from former friends. Look at what he says: "You long to see us, just as we also long to see you."

So often, when people are in a time of distress amidst afflictions, they tend to go to the other side of the street when they see someone familiar approaching. They don't want to answer their phone calls. They don't want to relate to anyone else. They want to be aloof, distant, isolated.

The worst place in the world to be, when going through doubts, is all alone. You need a friend—someone close, like a Jonathan—to support you. The Thessalonian Christians continued reaching out to Paul. They didn't isolate themselves even though their comfort zone had been invaded. They genuinely desired Paul's encouragement.

And third, they passed the final test as well: they had a firm commitment to spiritual truth.

For this reason, brethren, in all our distress and affliction we were comforted about you through your faith (v. 7).

There it is again. "We were so encouraged to know you're still believing in prayer, you're still trusting in God, you're still counting on Him to be glorified."

Now don't miss something that Paul quietly drops in toward the end of this paragraph. He says, *"For now we really live, if you stand firm in the Lord"* (v. 8).

Does that surprise anybody else? You'd think Paul had really lived no matter what. No, that's not true. Nothing helped him stand firm and *"really live"* like knowing his children in the faith were doing the same . . . in spite of affliction.

Practical Thoughts to Consider during Affliction

I want to point out a couple of things that I've been saving until now. These two truths will make all the difference, if you will keep them in mind when assaulted by affliction.

Number one: *As Christians, having our comfort zone invaded is essential . . . not unfair.*

You know a good example of that? The same reason people say, "It's best not to have just one child. It's better to have several in the family." Why? Because when you have brothers or sisters, they invade your comfort zone. They get under your skin. (They also get into your closet!) They have a way of dirtying dishes that you have to clean. They are notorious for messing up a house that you have to vacuum. And we who came from large families would agree that it was best—now that we look back. Rather than being unfair . . . it was essential.

Number two: *As soldiers, suffering hardship in battle is expected . . . not unusual.*

If you lived back in the days of the Second World War, as I did, you will remember a phrase that was often repeated: "There's a war on." Remember hearing that? Remember saying that? Someone would ask you about something you were doing that seemed a little extravagant. They would say, "How can you do that? There's a war on!"

I remember reading the gasoline rationing sticker that my dad had stuck on the right corner of the windshield of our car. It had a little statement on it that read, "Is this trip really necessary?" And with gasoline rationed as it was, if we were out just taking a drive and it looked like we weren't really going anywhere, someone had the right to say, "Why are you doing that? This trip isn't essential. There's a war on!" Restrictions and warfare go hand in hand. Suffering hardship is par for the course when we are traveling down the avenue of affliction.

Tertullian, in his *Address to Martyrs,* wrote, "No soldier comes to the war surrounded by luxuries, nor goes into action from a comfortable bedroom, but from the makeshift and narrow tent, where every kind of hardness and severity and unpleasantness is to be found." He understood the austerity that accompanies the battle.

I began with a quote from Scott Peck. I want to conclude with another one: "Truth ... is avoided when it is painful. We can revise our maps only when we have the discipline to overcome that pain. To have such discipline, we must be totally dedicated to truth. That is to say that we must always hold truth . . . to be more important, more vital to our self-interest, than our comfort. Conversely, we must always consider our personal discomfort relatively unimportant and, indeed, even welcome it in the service of the search for truth. . . . [And] what does a life of total dedication to the truth mean?" [Dr. Peck lists three essentials:] (1) "Continuous, and never-ending stringent self-examination." (2) "Willingness to be personally challenged." (3) "Total honesty." (None of these things comes painlessly!)[3]

God has used every means conceivable to get your attention. Perhaps He has not yet gotten it. He will not quit until He does. And He will bring you to a knowledge of the truth, as He invades your comfort zone and escorts you down the road less traveled.

For some of you who read this booklet, it means coming to faith in Christ. And you know it. You just can't dodge it any longer. Today is the day for you to submit to Him . . . today. Quit putting it off—there is no better time to turn to Him than today. For others, it means turning over the controls of your life to the Lord your God. It means full surrender.

Dear Father in heaven: Thank You for being faithful to us in the warfare. Thank You for taking away the luxuries of the bedroom and the comforts of the kitchen and the soft, padded carpet of the living room and for pushing us out into the streets. Thank You for the benefits of pain and suffering. Enable us to learn and never forget what You are teaching us; may we, in the truest sense of the word, *consider.*

May we, from this day forward, resist the temptation to avoid the pain when our comfort zone gets the squeeze. Rather, may we learn from it as we journey down the path of affliction. For Jesus' sake. Amen.

[1]A.W. Tozer, *Root of the Righteous* (Harrisburg: Christian Publications, Inc., 1955), p. 137.

[2]Gail MacDonald, *High Call, High Privilege* (Wheaton: Tyndale House Publishers, Inc., 1981), p. 29.

[3]M. Scott Peck, M.D., *The Road Less Traveled: A New Psychology of Love, Traditional Values, and Spiritual Growth* (New York: Touchstone Books, 1978), pp. 50-52, 56.